TRANSDEV BLAZEFIELD BUSES

SCOTT POOLE

AMBERLEY

Acknowledgements

Again, I would like to thank everyone at Amberley books, especially Connor Stait, who has been very helpful during the planning of the books. Also, thanks to Sarah for organising the blogs used on the Amberley website.

It has been another interesting trip down nostalgia road, looking at the various buses which have been used across the Transdev/Blazefield network. I hope everyone enjoys this book as much as I have enjoyed compiling notes and sorting out the photographs.

I would like to dedicate this book to the drivers, fitters, cleaners, service delivery crews and the Transdev management team, for their hard work and dedication to the job of getting us, the passengers, to work, home, that party and, of course, out to meet friends or just out enjoying the views.

Thank you, now sit back with a cuppa/brew and enjoy.

First published 2020

Amberley Publishing
The Hill, Stroud
Gloucestershire, GL5 4EP

www.amberley-books.com

Copyright © Scott Poole, 2020

The right of Scott Poole to be identified as
the Author of this work has been asserted in
accordance with the Copyrights, Designs and
Patents Act 1988.

ISBN 978 1 4456 9720 8 (print)
ISBN 978 1 4456 9721 5 (ebook)

British Library Cataloguing in Publication Data.
A catalogue record for this book is available from
the British Library.

Origination by Amberley Publishing.
Printed in the UK.

Introduction

Transdev arrived, in a big way, in the UK during 2006, purchasing the Northern-based former Blazefield bus operations. Then, in 2008, it acquired the operations of Veolia, based in York. This book concentrates on the bus fleets in Lancashire and Yorkshire as the main area of operations for the North. Investment was slow to commence during 2006–2015, as the company was containing the services in reasonable order. Investment saw a new fleet of Optare Versa saloons in Burnley, in 2007, for the Starship brand, and nineteen new Volvo B7RLE/Wrightbus Eclipse saloons for the Mainline in Burnley, new in 2009. Harrogate got eight Optare Versa saloons in 2012, plus two for Burnley. For 2005 and 2009 Yorkshire Coastliner got two batches of Volvo B7TL and B9TL/Wrightbus Gemini double-deckers. These were joined by two more batches in 2011 and 2012, while Burnley got fifteen new Volvo B9TLs with Wrightbus Gemini bodies for the rebranded WitchWay service, just in time for Halloween in October 2013. 2015 brought a new direction and management team into the Transdev Blazefield company, including high-profile changes, with 'revitalised' buses for key services in Keighley, Harrogate and in Blackburn and Burnley. A new era for double-deck travel arrived at Harrogate in early 2016 as the 36 was rebranded as 'Riding Redefined'. Then Yorkshire Coastliner gained ten new vehicles for its routes in 2017, plus three more in 2018. All these new buses are on the Volvo B5TL with Wrightbus Gemini 3 bodywork.

Blackburn and Burnley got more new Optare Versa saloons – eighteen for the 6 and 7 in Blackburn, in 2016, and thirty for the new look Mainline in 2017 – plus five new ADL E20Ds for York in 2019. New local identities were introduced during 2016 and 2017 for each area, along with simpler tickets, such as the Day Tripper ticket. Perhaps the most successful achievement was the purchase of the Rosso Bus operation from Rossendale Council. In just over sixteen months, with a £3,000,000 investment in fourteen new Optare Versa saloons, the 'revitalised' buses for new and improved routes around the Greater Manchester area. Rosso has had the most prolific year as it transforms and improves its service. Passenger numbers have increased across the network of the services, all seeing around a 4 per cent plus rise on the average year on year figures. The York-based CityZap saw its 250,000th customer before its first year had finished. The high-profile routes, such as the 36 and the Coastliner services, saw an average 97 per cent passenger satisfaction in the level of service. Investment is set to continue into 2020, with thirteen new ADL E20D saloons for the number 1 in Blackburn and a new fleet of buses for the York City Zap, with new buses being trialed across the year – with more new ideas and innovation for passengers in 2020, it's going to be another busy year. To finish off this introduction, the newest bus station in the UK at the time of writing is due to open in the town of Rawtenstall in November 2019.

Transdev Blazefield A History

AJS Holdings

As part of the 1985 Transport Act, which was known as deregulation, times were changing for the National Bus Company (NBC), which had to prepare its subsidiaries to be sold off, either as management buyouts or into new groups. The companies operating within the commercial boundaries and restrictions of deregulation.

AJS Holdings purchased West Yorkshire Road Car Company in August 1987 and used this opportunity to split the company into smaller operating divisions – Harrogate & District, Keighley & District, York City & District, West Yorkshire (operating from Bradford) and Leeds & Otley. In January 1990 the Malton depot became part of the new Yorkshire Coastliner operation, which linked the east coast with Leeds and York. However, a big shock arrived during August 1989 when Rider Holdings managed to acquire the remaining part of the West Yorkshire Road Car Company. In March 1990, the operations in Bradford, Leeds and Otley were absorbed into the Yorkshire Rider fleet; the former WYRCC depots were not included with the sale. Then, in July 1990, the operations in York including York City, Reynard Pullman and Target Travel were merged as Rider Holdings purchased the lot. It was at this time owner Alan Stephenson decided to sell his quarter share in AJS to a new company created in 1991.

Blazefield Holdings

The new company was created by Mr Giles Freanley and Mr Stuart Wilde, both former West Yorkshire RCC employees, who took over the Yorkshire companies along with their operating units that worked in London and Cambridge. One of their initial moves in the company was to introduce new branding on key routes, with a simple livery, which saw an increase in passenger numbers.

Expansion arrived in 2001, when an unexpected purchase was on the table as the former Stagecoach East Lancashire operations in Bolton, Blackburn, Burnley and Clitheroe were acquired. This led to Stagecoach cascading unwanted buses into the Lancashire operation. Over sixty new buses for Burnley and Blackburn were ordered for delivery during 2001/2. The Bolton services and depot were sold to Blue Bus of Horwich. Between 2002 and 2005, the southern-based units were sold off: London Sovereign to Transdev, Huntingdon & District to Cavalier Travel in 2003 with the St Albans operation going to Centre Bus in 2004. The remaining Sovereign operation was eventually sold to Arriva after clearance by the Competition Commission in 2005.

During 2005/6 Blazefield were approached by the French-owned Transdev company, who made offers for the company. However, in 2006, a deal was struck and Blazefield was acquired by Transdev.

Transdev

The French-based company was soon to expand the Blackburn fleet with the purchase of Accrington Transport, Blackburn Transport and Northern Blue in 2007. A new network name, Spot-On, was introduced in the Blackburn area with a new livery and some new buses. Northern Blue would remain as a separate company until 2010, when absorbed into the Burnley fleet.

In York, Veolia Transport had won the tenders for services within the city in 2006. They worked with Top Line Travel and shared the depot in Fulford, York. August 2008 saw Transdev expand into York with the purchase of the Veolia business. By 2012 the York Pullman stage carriage service and open-top bus tours were acquired too. However, in 2016, York lost the university tender to First York. Finally, in December 2017 the council-owned Rosso Bus was acquired by Transdev, which was finalised in early 2018.

In this book the author will concentrate on the period from 1991 until 2019, as the Blazefield company (later Transdev) brought in branding, customer feedback information and improvements not only to services but the vehicles as well.

The current business has seen the construction of a new, younger management team, along with a fresh new marketing division. This commenced with the introduction of Mr Alex Hornby, who had left Trent-Barton to join the company, in 2015. It was during this period that the marketing team was also changed into a younger team. Transdev Blazefield also opened its depots across the company for the public and enthusiasts to have an opportunity to look behind the scenes of the operations. These proved very popular indeed. Much-needed investment was provided, starting with the revitalised look to the 662 Shuttle service from Bradford to Keighley, in late 2015. This was quickly followed by the Riding Redefined 36 project, again seeing pioneering improvements to the whole concept of bus travel.

Local identities for each division were also key, so during 2016 liveries were brought out for each area: the Burnley Bus Company – two-tone orange; the Blackburn Bus Company – two-tone blue; the Harrogate Bus Company – two-tone red; the Keithley Bus Company – two-tone green; Coastliner and York & Country – both two-tone blue; Rosso Bus – no new livery, but new brands within the fleet.

Burnley & Pendle

The towns of Burnley, Colne and Nelson all operated vehicles as separate companies. Burnley began, in 1901, to run trams. Later, in 1924, motorbuses were introduced on some selected routes. Buses ran outside of the borough boundary from 1921 for the first time. By 1935 the final tram journeys were concluded, running to Nelson. Nelson began its tramway in 1903 and by 1923 the first local bus services commenced. With the buses proving popular, the last tram trip was in early 1934.

Colne was the smaller operator and the last to introduce trams, late in 1903. By 1911, all three companies' tramways ran into each district. Like Nelson, the Colne tramway closed in 1934. Buses arrived in the 1920s and continued to grow.

In 1933, Burnley, Colne and Nelson were joined together and formed the BCN Joint Transport. A new livery of maroon and cream was used, and various vehicles purchased.

1974 saw the creation of Burnley & Pendle, because of local government reorganisation. Burnley continued beyond the 1985 Transport Act and continued to provide local bus services.

In 1997 Stagecoach managed a 50 per cent share in the company, but this led to strained relations. In 2001 Stagecoach sold Burnley to Blazefield, who reversed the fortunes of the depot. Today the company is part of the Transdev operation, as The Burnley Bus Company uses a two-tone orange base livery. A modern low-floor fleet of buses keeps the town moving ahead with the Mainline and the WitchWay brands.

After the sale of the East Lancashire depots was complete, Stagecoach was able to cascade unwanted vehicles into the fleet. Here 165, a former Stagecoach South Plaxton-bodied Dennis Javelin, pauses on Manchester Road on a local service.

The MCW Metrobus, along with Leyland Atlanteans, had a very short stay with the new Burnley & Pendle company. Here 1225 starts its journey towards the Stoops Estate. The bus was sold on for further service. It was eventually sold for preservation in 2009 and has been repainted into the Greater Manchester PTE livery.

Former Ribble NBC standard specification double-deckers were the main vehicle type in the Burnley fleet, like 2101, which is seen in the old-style bus station. This Olympian has become part of the Ribble Vehicle Preservation Trust fleet, having been kept by Blazefield chairman Giles Fearnley. 2101 has been a regular rally attendant since its restoration in 2008.

Relatively new buses were also cascaded into the Burnley fleet, like this Volvo B6BLE with Alexander ALX200 bodywork. It is seen here in the new-look Burnley livery with scroll-style fleetname.

The Volvo B10M-55 with Alexander PS bodywork was the standard saloon for every Stagecoach fleet. This bus was part of a batch of fifteen vehicles new in 1995 that found their way into the Burnley fleet. This one is working the Pike Hill service.

June 2001 brought in the new vehicles ordered by Blazefield for Burnley, twenty-five in total. These Wrightbus-bodied Volvo B10BLEs were used to promote the new-look Mainline brand. Here 1042 stands in Burnley, St James Street, fresh out of the box.

Sixteen new Volvo B7TL/Plaxton Presidents also arrived in June 2001, taking on the former Ribble X43 Manchester service. These new vehicles were branded using a stylised Pendle Witch on a broomstick. 2701 pauses at Grassington on a Sunday extension of the Witch Way service, for the summer DalesBus season.

In 1988 two Volvo B10M-50s with Alexander RV bodies and coach seating arrived into Burnley stock. Here 1301 is seen heading for Preston, having been repainted into the new Burnley livery.

1105 was one of two former Volvo B7L demonstrator buses bought by Burnley during 2003. The other was 1104, which had spent a short time working the 36 in Harrogate during early 2002. Here on St James Street in Burnley, 1105 loads passengers for Rosegrove, an area outside of Burnley town. Both 1104 and 1105 were later transferred to Blackburn in 2007 for the Spot-On routes in the city.

Investment for the latest vehicles to work the X43/44 services arrived in 2005 with fifteen Volvo B7TLs/Wrightbuses with Gemini bodywork. They used the 36 livery and WitchWay branding, as shown by 2762 named *Margaret Pearson*, one of the Pendle Witches.

February 2008 saw the delivery of nineteen Optare Versa saloons, numbers 251–269, introduced with the new Starship local livery. Here 261 enters Red Lion Street working the 101 to Pike Hill on 7 May 2009. During a service review, the Starship network was numbered from 1 to 12 in 2012/13.

Nine of the original batch of Volvo B10BLE/Wrightbus Mainline saloons, numbers 1042–72 (1042, 43, 46, 53, 58, 62, 71 and 72), were treated to a refurb in 2010. Here, 1062 is seen working into Clitheroe, in Burnley, in the 2009 brand and livery.

In 2014 Burnley acquired nine new Wrightbus integral Streetlite DF versions to work on the local network of routes. 604 heads towards Rosegrove Lane Ends after visiting the Boundary Mill outlet near Colne. The Streetlites also introduced the Burnley Connect livery and brand, using similar colours to the Mainline 2009 livery.

In 2012 two more Versas joined the Burnley ranks, numbers 285–6, arriving in the Starship livery. Here 286 turns into Manchester Road working the 1 to Stoops Estate. However, 286 would gain a new livery during 2015, the Burnley Connect livery.

In 2009 the Mainline was given a boost with nineteen brand new Volvo B7RLEs with Wrightbus bodywork, a new livery and branding. Here 1853, the first of the batch, enters Red Lion Street working the 29 to Barnoldswick, on 7 May 2009.

Halloween 2013 saw the delivery of fifteen brand new Volvo B9TLs, with Wrightbus Gemini 2 double-decker bodies, for a refresh and rebrand of the Witch Way. Here 2766 climbs towards Manchester across the tops, having just left Burnley on the first day of service. Bus 2776 was used in the town centre to introduce the new WitchWay brand with some goodie bags and new timetables.

Following the introduction of the new WitchWay vehicles, the older vehicles were being prepared for continued service with enhanced route branding. Here 2750 is seen working the Mainline service 29 in the North Yorkshire town of Skipton, in the full Mainline livery and branding, on 11 April 2016.

In order to simplify the Mainline numbers, Burnley looked to reduce the numbers and replace the Skipton Mainline routes with an extension of the X43 to Skipton. 1071 departs Whalley after visiting Clitheroe as the M2. The M1 went to Barnoldswick; the M3 to Trawden and Accrington; and the M4 to Keighley.

During December 2016, Transdev announced they were requiring passenger feedback for the new-look Mainline vehicles. The 'Make My Mainline' tag line, which saw an award from *Route One* magazine in 2018, allowed the Burnley public to bring ideas to the table. 258 is one of thirty new Optare Versa integral saloons, purchased for the route, seen here departing Clitheroe on the first Monday in service.

The new Mainline vehicles had many interesting features, which are now standard on all Transdev's new and revitalised vehicles: dual-purpose seating, improved legroom, USB power, wireless charging, glazed ceiling panels and free Wi-Fi. 266, which is seen on the first Monday of operation passing through Laneshawbridge, is Burnley bound having just visited Keighley on the M4 service.

November 2017 saw an ambitious venture with buses travelling from Leeds city to Manchester city centre via the busy M62 motorway. Using four revitalised Volvo B7RLEs with Wrightbus Eclipse bodies, numbers 1868–1871 were painted into the CityZap livery, along with the addition of many standard Transdev features including quilted leather seats. Here 1870 is passing through Ainley Top on a very sunny day during the first week of operation.

Because of other plans for Burnley's Streetlites, it was necessary to repaint a selection of the Volvo B10BLEs into the new Burnley livery. Here, 1072 is seen entering Melville Street from Thorsby Road on 21 March 2018. Working the 2 service to Higherford, outside of Colne, 1072 would also be reregistered as B10 TDV.

So far seven former Mainline Volvo B10BLEs have been repainted as well as getting a spring clean before entering service. 1046 is seen working the 3 Pike Hill service on 8 October 2018. Numbers 1042, 1043, 1046, 1058, 1071–72 and 1086 have been treated this way. At the time of writing 1053 was also being prepped for service for the local Burnley routes.

The Manchester to Leeds CityZap started off very well with the first week bringing in over 1,500 passengers, especially at £1 per trip. The interest continued to grow, but the M62 was the devil in the detail with its heavy use and troublesome junctions in West Yorkshire. Despite the best endeavors of the team of Burnley drivers, in the end it was the accidents, delays and various factors that brought the Manchester CityZap to an untimely end. 1869 is seen about to head towards Leeds, having just passed through Ainley Top, on the penultimate day of operation, Friday 20 July 2018.

Harrogate & District

Harrogate began in 1906 using a single Clarkson steam-powered bus. By 1907 more steam buses arrived. During the next few years the services grew and expanded. Harrogate added 'Road Car' to its title, with interest from Thomas Tilling during 1924, later adding 'and District' to the name. By 1928, having purchased Blythe & Berwick, Bradford and also absorbing Premier Travel of Keighley, Harrogate became West Yorkshire Road Car (WYRCC). Interest was shown from two railway companies in 1929, the LMS and LNER, who acquired shares.

The coaching era arrived in the 1930s and 1940s, as West Yorkshire, along with other operators, formed coaching services around the country. By 1942, Tilling had gained all the shares in the company, only to see it change hands in 1948 with nationalization. WYRCC were owned by the British Transport Commission. WYRCC continued into the new era, with joint working on the 36, which began in 1926 with United. The swinging sixties arrived and saw WYRCC change ownership twice.

As part of the National Bus Company in 1969, West Yorkshire still had the Bristol/ECW vehicles along with new Leyland vehicles. It all ended in 1987 when WYRCC was purchased by AJS Holdings. In 1991 Blazefield took over the Harrogate & District operation. In 2006 Transdev brought Blazefield and have continued to provide some new styles to the fleet. Today as the Harrogate Bus Company, with a red livery and new brands, it continues to bring a much-improved network of services, along with fourteen new high-specification vehicles for the 36.

The summer of 1990, as Harrogate & District operate from the Leeds Central bus station, due to the closure of Vicar Lane in March 1990. Here 302 is seen about to head to Wetherby in a West Yorkshire livery, but with Harrogate & District fleetnames.

The Leyland National Mk 2 was introduced around 1978/9 and proved the model's own salvation, using the powerful Leyland 0.680 engine as standard. Here a former WYRCC example is seen as Harrogate 336 working an evening turn on the 24 to Pateley Bridge.

Still in the post-1986 West Yorkshire dual-purpose livery is this Duple-bodied Leyland Leopard coach, No. 683, one of two similar vehicles in the Harrogate fleet. The coach is parked on Station Parade during the summer of 1992, when the former bus station was closed. Eventually, after being turned into a car park, sanity returned to the area and the car park turned back to a bus station in the late 1990s.

The Leyland Lynx arrived into Harrogate in 1986 with two examples, numbers 1201–2, later becoming 324–325. In 1988 six more Lynx saloons arrived as 203–208 then as 373–78. By 1989 the final four Lynxes arrived as 381–84; these had dual-purpose seating and were used on the 36 service, as seen here with 383 picking up passengers in the summer of 1990 in Leeds Central bus station.

Harrogate also ordered two small batches of minibuses for delivery in 1989 and 1990. Seen here in York, pausing on Rougier Street, is 276, one of the Iveco 49:10s with Reeve Burgess bodywork. Harrogate bought numbers 275–281. The 1990 minibuses were Renault/Dodge S56s with Reeve Burgess bodies; these were numbered 291–294.

From 1994 Blazefield used Volvo chassis as its main choice, initially with Alexander bodywork and then standardising on Wrightbus bodies. Here 650, a Volvo B6B with Alexander Dash bodywork, is seen on Station Parade when pressed into service in 1994 without fleetnames, numbers or branding.

With Volvo purchasing the remaining parts of the Leyland bus business, in 1993, Volvo pressed its versatile B10B-58 chassis. Here is 363, one of five Volvo B10B-58s with Alexander Strider bodywork, new in 1995. The bus is seen on Briggate, Leeds, about to head for Ripon, in the post-1993 livery and route branding.

Following on from the 1994 delivery of ten Volvo B6Bs were numbers 676–679, later 664–667. These midibuses were branded for the 78 Harrogate–Wetherby–Boston Spa and Tadcaster service. 678 stands on Station Parade in front of a National and Olympian, with the temporary car park to the right.

From 1996 until 2002 Blazefield purchased the Volvo B10B chassis for its single-deck fleet. Numbers 366–368 arrived in 1996, for the 36 service, with dual-purpose seats and the branding for the service. Here 368 is about to turn into King's Road from Skipton Road. Harrogate buses that ventured into Leeds had Metro stickers applied.

641, which is seen in the post-1996 redeveloped Ripon bus station, was new in 1997 and was Harrogate's first low-floor vehicle. Part of a batch of three Volvo B6BLEs with Wrightbus Crusader bodywork, 641 also has a Metro sticker as this bus was also used on the Leeds–Wetherby–Harrogate route.

Investment to replace the Alexander/Volvo midibuses arrived in June 2000 with fourteen new Volvo B6BLEs with Wrightbus Crusader bodies. Here 608 is collecting customers from Slatergate roundabout before the bus turns round, heading back to Harrogate. The 103 was the new service number from 15 April 2001.

Also arriving in 2000 and 2002 were batches of the low-floor Volvo B10BLE with Wrightbus bodywork. Numbers 301–304 were initially used across the network before settling on the 36. Numbers 305–309 were employed on 36 duties in January 2002 because of a strike on the trains. Here 309 sports the Burnley red livery with 101/102 branding.

November 2002 saw a return to buses for Skipton, this time with funding by Travel Links and the Rural Bus Challenge run on behalf of North Yorkshire County Council. The service started on 4 November 2002. A few days later 704 is seen at Kettlesing Head, setting off for Skipton.

With the arrival of the twenty-five Volvo/Wrightbus saloons for the Mainline in Burnley, the Dennis Javelins with Plaxton bodywork were redundant. However, with a contract won by Harrogate & District for school transport, the coaches were given a lick of paint and up seated to sixty. 140 demonstrates the new look on a wet September morning in 2002.

Ripley in North Yorkshire is the location for this at the time on loan Volvo B7RLE with Wrightbus Eclipse body. This vehicle stayed with Harrogate for a while from April to May 2003. It was then used as a demonstrator, before returning to Harrogate as 1700.

27 October 2003 saw the maiden voyage of the new line of twin-decks on the 36 service, as 3601 entered into traffic. 3601 had her debut at the 2003 NEC Bus & Coach show that year, sparking much interest amongst the visitors at the show. Here the bus is seen at Pannal Spacey Houses during her first week of operation. Numbers 3602–12 would join 3601 during March and April 2004, lasting until early 2016.

March 2004 saw more investment into the Knaresborough Road service with five new Volvo B7RLEs with Wrightbus Eclipse bodywork, numbers 1701–5. Here 1703 departs Harrogate on 17 August 2004 in full branding and the Burnley-style red livery, introduced to Harrogate during 2002.

March 2004 also saw the arrival of 1800, which was originally painted into the 36 livery and used on the quieter journeys of the 36. By 2006 the bus was regularly seen working the 100–102 services. 1800 is seen here on 15 March 2007, working the 100 to Aspin in the Keighley Shuttle livery with Transdev fleet names.

During February 2010, Volvo B7RLEs 1701–02 were given a midlife overhaul with new seats and a new livery of butterscotch and burgundy. Here 1701 has paused in the bus station in Knaresborough on 13 February 2010 after being unveiled. The new-look branding and slogans finish off the whole image nicely.

In March 2010, Volvo B10BLE/Wrightbus numbers 307 and 309 were also given midlife overhauls, but they were diverted from the Knaresborough Road services. They were branded for the relaunch of the Pateley Bridge 24 service as the Nidderdale branch. 307 is seen at Birstwith working its way back to Harrogate on a wet March day.

In September 2010, one of the former WitchWay Volvo/Plaxton double-deckers arrived from its midlife overhaul with the double-deck version of the new Harrogate livery. 2708 is seen on New Briggate, in Leeds, about to pick up passengers for a countryside trip towards Harrogate via Wetherby. Note its dedicated 770 route branding.

Harrogate tried two hybrid demonstrators from ADL and Volvo for evaluation for fuel and reliability and to compare in tests against the 2003/4 Volvo B7TL/Wrightbus buses. 2706 was given an extensive overhaul and interior redesign with six single seats on the upper deck and a lounge area in the rear lower saloon. As the ideas in action bus, 2706 was sent into service on the 36 routes for passenger feedback.

May 2011 saw the return of 3601, which had been given a substantial overhaul, with new engine, cooling system, new updated front end, full rear destination screen and the new-look interior design. The new livery and City Connect branding made the 36 stand out from the crowd. Later Wi-Fi would be added to the fleet. Here 3601 is seen at Ripley Cross, having just entered revenue earning service.

The fourteen Volvo B6BLE/Wrightbus midibuses were going to be replaced by eight new Optare Versa saloons, which arrived in May 2012. Numbers 277–284 were placed into service along with a few refinements for the passengers. Plus, these buses had another new Harrogate livery of red and black, painted in a corporate style. Here 277, on her fifth day in service, turns into Knox Lane from Bachelor Gardens working the 2B.

Three years after being repainted into the butterscotch and burgundy livery, 1701 sports the Harrogate Connect livery. Here 1701 is seen on Park Row, Knaresborough, working the 1C to Carmires estate. Transdev certainly know how to keep the whole fleet fresh with interesting liveries and branding on the major routes. The number 1 service between Harrogate and Knaresborough had eye-catching branding.

1084 was one of four former Lancashire United Volvo/Wrightbus saloons to be transferred across to Harrogate in 2007, along with numbers 1085–7. Here it is seen working the 770 via Follifoot and Spofforth, passing Rudding Park in the Harrogate Connect livery.

Harrogate had trialed the Optare Solo SR-EV in October 2013, placing an order for two Solo SR-EVs. York had theirs delivered first. By April 2014, the solitary example for Harrogate arrived. It was used to promote 'Catch a bus week' in the town. Here the bus is seen working the X6 express service to Beckwith Knowle on a morning journey.

During 2015, Transdev had placed an order for fourteen high-specification long-wheelbase Volvo B5TLs with new Wrightbus Gemini 3 bodywork. Here 3619 is seen in Ripon during the first week of operation, looking resplendent in the new 'Riding Redefined' livery. Features include double glazing, glazed ceiling panels, airline-style upper saloon seating, quilted leather lower saloon seating, rear saloon tables, small tables upstairs, free Wi-Fi, USB power, a library, and next stop audio/visual announcements.

Harrogate was in the process of repainting the fleet again, three years after introducing the Harrogate Connect livery. This time a pleasing two-tone red livery was designed as the Harrogate Bus Company was introduced, harking back to the Tilling red of WYRCC. Here 3614, formerly 2765 of Lancashire United, is Ripon bound.

Numbers 1834, 37, 38 and 39 were withdrawn from Blackburn and were revitalised in-house by the ESU unit at Intack. All four buses were overhauled with new front ends, improved seats, next stop audio and visual announcements, free Wi-Fi and at-seat USB power. Here 1837 is seen at High Bridge, Knaresborough, outside of Mother Shipton's, Harrogate bound.

Former Burnley Mainline saloons numbers 1853–62 were also given the Transdev treatment with new seats, USB power, free Wi-Fi and audio/visual next stop announcements. Here 1854 is seen in Thorner, a village outside of Leeds, in the new livery with the seven-number logo, after a brief spell as the 70/71 service.

Early in February 2017, Harrogate announced to bring into service eight high-specification Volvo 7900EVs for use on the local routes around Harrogate, replacing the 2012 Optare Versa saloons. After a Stakeholders' event, held at Betty's Tea Rooms, the buses were used on an extended proving period with driver training and route learning as the electric buses are 12 metres in length. A pilot running experiment led to short-term generator assistance. In early 2019, with all the issues now sorted, the new electric generator was switched on. Here 807 is seen on Knox Avenue working the 2B back to Harrogate. At the UK Bus Awards in November 2019, the Harrogate electrics won the Environment Innovation Award Gold at a special event in the Troxy, London.

Keighley & District

During 1889 the Keighley Tramways Company commenced operation of a horse-drawn service. 1901 saw the local borough council purchasing this concern. Services continued until the permission to use electrification for the system was duly allowed in 1904. By 1913 Keighley began using 'trackless' buses, which served the town and outlying areas, such as Utley and Stockbridge. However, the trackless buses were considered somewhat unreliable and the Corporation turned to the motorbus from 1921.

The tramway was abandoned in 1924, this saw an increase in the use of the trolleybus. It was around this time that West Yorkshire Road Car were slowly acquiring local transport operations. Agreements were sought after to enable a joint working partnership. Keighley then continued to work with WYRCC and in 1928 saw more Leyland double-deck vehicles arrive.

Finally, in 1932, with all issues and concerns addressed, WYRCC took control of the Keighley Corporation, which became known as Keighley West Yorkshire. By 1969 K-WYRCC became part of the NBC, which by 1973 saw the Keighley operation absorbed into the main West Yorkshire fleet, as the new West Yorkshire PTE and new Metropolitan Council were created.

By 1987, AJS holdings had bought WYRCC and then split the company into smaller units. Keighley & District was formed, joining Blazefield in 1991 and then Transdev in 2006. Today with a modern fleet of buses, the Keighley Bus Company continues to provide a network of services with some dedicated branded routes.

A former West Yorkshire B-series integral Leyland National is seen paused at the old Keighley bus station during the early 1990s. 258 is waiting a turn on the 719, a local service to Brackenbank. The B-series Nationals were employed on routes which required a lighter vehicle.

A former West Yorkshire Bristol VRT is seen standing in Ilkley, working the 762 service to Keighley, way back in 1989. 318, which was once part of 170 Bristol VRT/ECW double-deckers in the WYRCC fleet, only had a brief stay with Keighley. The bus is seen in the old poppy red livery with the addition of the chinchilla grey stripe.

A former West Yorkshire Leyland Olympian with ECW bodywork, which succeeded the Bristol VRT as the NBC standard double-decker from 1982. Here 361, seen arriving into the old Leeds Central bus station, sports one of many livery variations used by Keighley.

West Yorkshire used the Leyland Leopard coach chassis with either Plaxton or, as seen here on 232, Duple bodywork for National Express work. This coach is seen in Keighley and is about to be driven back to the depot after a day's duty. Yet again another version of the chinchilla grey livery is used on 232.

Six Northern Counties-bodied Leyland Olympians arrived in 1990, numbers 331–336, all of which had roller blind destination screens. Here 332, seen in Bradford working a private charter, has had its original destination screen replaced with an electronic version. Like other Keighley buses, 332 sports another version of the chinchilla and red livery.

202, an integral Leyland Lynx, is parked at Leeds while working the 760 service. It is part of a batch of eight vehicles which arrived in 1989. The Lynxes were used to improve the profile of this trunk route between Leeds and Keighley via Shipley.

Keighley based its Northern Rose operation in the town, operating private charters and other coaching work. 242, seen dispatching passengers having travelled from Colne, in Lancashire, was part of the West Yorkshire coaching fleet. New in 1983, this is a Leyland Tiger with Plaxton bodywork.

During 1992, Keighley had decided to revise the livery used by the company, giving a fresh feel and a new, crisp look. Olympian 388 is seen in Leeds sporting the new and brighter livery while on 760 duty. Later in 1994 the grey areas were painted blue and again there were some variations to the scheme.

Keighley 101, a Plaxton Beaver-bodied Mercedes-Benz 711D, was one of eight minibuses delivered in 1993. It was followed by five more later in 1993. These were the longer 811D version with Plaxton bodies. 101 is seen heading for Silsden in the so called 'Big K' livery.

Keighley acquired three Alexander Dash-bodied Volvo B6Bs as numbers 221–223. Harrogate had ten delivered of the same type, also delivered in 1994. Here 222 is seen in a later adaptation of the 1994 livery with larger fleetnames, with colours applied in a similar manner to the Burnley red livery.

1996 brought more new Volvo vehicles into Keighley stock, by which time the former West Yorkshire vehicles were withdrawn or had become part of the schools bus fleet. Here 501, the first of ten Alexander Strider-bodied Volvo B10Bs, is seen here in Ilkley working the 762 service via Addingham, Steeton and Silsden.

Also delivered in 1996 were five Volvo B10Bs with Wrightbus bodywork, which became the standard for the whole group. Here 514, the penultimate batch member, is seen working the branded 669 Keighley to Airedale Hospital service. By the year 2000, numbers 511–515 were transferred across to Harrogate.

Keighley purchased its last Leyland Olympians in 1993, the same year Volvo acquired this once mighty manufacturer. 902 was one of four Alexander R-type-bodied vehicles, which were used on the 760 Leeds service. Here, as the bus travels along the Headrow, in Leeds, the branding for the 760 can be seen.

New to Yorkshire Coastliner in 1995 as numbers 422–425, this batch of Alexander Royale-bodied Volvo Olympians were moved across to Keighley in 2000. Here 923, one of four buses, is paused awaiting departure at the redesigned Leeds City bus station. The bus also sports another variation of the blue livery with Airelink 760 branding.

From 1998 until 2000 Keighley purchased thirty-five low-floor Volvo B10BLEs, with Wright Renown bodywork, in three batches numbering 521–31, 540–551 and 557–77. 550, from the second batch, is seen in Bradford working the 662 service with full branding for the Airedale Shuttle.

In 2004, Keighley wanted to refresh the local network of services 701–720 with the introduction of the Zone. Trans-Bus Darts were purchased for use on these routes and were painted into a blue and red livery. The Darts arrived as numbers 706–720 and certainly stood out from the rest of the fleet. Here 714 returns from working at the circular 703 Braithwaite service.

In April 2005, Blazefield ordered a batch of fourteen new Volvo B7RLE with Wright Eclipse bodywork. Numbers 1801–1814 arrived with a new dedicated livery and branding for 'the Shuttle', the Bradford 662 service. Here 1808 is seen on a wet 9 May 2009, returning to Keighley.

During May 2010 the fourteen vehicles on the 662 service were treated to a new-look butterscotch and blue livery, along with new branding. Here 1807 is seen arriving at the Bradford Interchange on 19 May 2010. The Shuttle vehicles retained their dual-purpose leather seating for this new look.

In April 2008, eight more new Volvo B7RLE/Wrightbus saloons arrived as numbers 1843–1850 with a sweeping blue with white livery. 1844 is seen in Skipton bus station working the 66 to Keighley on 20 April 2010.

389, a former West Yorkshire Olympian, might well have been the last WYRCC vehicle in service. Here 389 is seen outside of Bradley, a village to the west of Keighley, working a peak-time service. The bus is in the final blue and white livery before the introduction of the 2010 green and blue livery.

Having spent its formative years working the Mainline services in Burnley, 1044 found her way across the Pennines to work in Keighley. Here 1044 is heading back into the town centre during a flurry of snow after visiting Stanbury, outside of Haworth. 1044 arrived at Keighley in 2009 and stayed until 2014, eventually being transferred to Blackburn.

Transdev acquired two Wrightbus integral Streetlites for use on the 500 Keighley to Hebden Bridge; numbers 610 and 611 arrived in February 2015. Here 611 is depicted in Haworth turning towards Sun Street before continuing towards Hebden Bridge. However, both Streetlites were transferred to Burnley, in 2017, and then Rosso, in March 2018.

During 2015–16 the 2005 Volvo B7RLEs/Wrightbus Eclipses, numbered 1801–14, were given a fresh new revitalised overhaul into the new 'Shuttle' look. Built in-house at the ESU in Blackburn, 1801–14 were given Mk 2 front ends, new interiors, USB power, Wi-Fi and a new brand and livery. Here 1804 is seen in Cottingley, working towards Keighley, in late 2015 while the new look was being launched by Transdev.

2016 saw the introduction of the new rebrand of the 66 as the DalesWay service between Keighley and Skipton. Officially launched in early September 2016 at Skipton town hall and later in Keighley, here 241, one of the three dedicated Optare Versa saloons acquired for the route, is seen turning in the village of Sutton during a wet spell of weather.

New to Yorkshire Coastliner in 2005, this was revitalised Volvo B7RLE/Wrightbus number 452. It was acquired by Yorkshire Coastlienr after a spell in Harrogate for the X54 service. All the buses were eventually brought together at Keighley. Here 452 is seen in Pecket Well, near the village pub, working the B3, formerly the 500 Hebden Bridge service. The Brontë Bus brand was introduced during 2015 for the 664, 665 and the 500, which were all renumbered in 2018 as the B1–3 Brontë Bus.

1848 was the first of the 2008 batch of Volvo B7RLE/Wrightbus saloons to gain the two-tone green Keighley livery. During 2016, as numbers 450–454 were revitalised, Keighley introduced the much-improved two-tone green livery. Newer vehicle deliveries arrived into the fleet in the new colours. 2708, 2716, 403 and 404 are so far the only double-deckers repainted into the new livery.

2018 saw Keighley return to Grassington as Pride of the Dales called time on working the 72 service from Skipton. Here 204 is seen arriving into Grassington during the first week of operation in April 2018. Later, in October 2018, Burnley withdrew from working the Sunday extensions on the X43. Keighley were quick to take over the 72 Sunday service, using a Keighley Jet liveried Optare Solo.

Former Yorkshire Coastliner 403 is seen sporting the new Keighley Bus Company two-tone green livery, while working the 760 main service from Leeds. This bus, along with 401–2 and 404, was loaned to Harrogate during 2010 for the 36 City Connect overhaul programme.

In 2016 and 2017 Keighley acquired two batches of integral Optare Solo minibuses for use on local services. These new buses replaced the Transbus Darts that were new in 2004 on the local services. Here 160, new in 2017, is seen in the new local brand the Keighley Jets. It is working the K6 Fell Lane service.

During 2018 Keighley regained some former routes after service retendering, awarded from Bradford-based TLC. The routes were renumbered as the K9–19. These services were of a very rural nature with the rural roads to match. Here 53 is seen working the first Sunday K14 Oxenhope–Keighley, which is the only K10–19 Sunday operation. 53 is seen in the village of Laycock during the first afternoon of service.

October 2017 saw the introduction of the four new Optare Versa saloons for the rebranding of the main service between Keighley and Leeds via Shipley, the 760 service. The Aireline 60 launch was based at the Victoria Gardens, in Keighley. Metro, Transdev and local councilors were invited. The buses have all the main Transdev features of new seats, improved legroom, USB power, Wi-Fi, wireless charging tables and next stop audio/visual announcements. Some workings have double-deckers working the service, with a Wrightbus integral Streetdeck Hybrid demonstrator in December 2018. The results so far have seen more Keighley livered double-deckers being used on the peak time diagrams.

Lancashire United

Starting with Ribble way back in 1919, these East Lancashire depots, in the areas of Blackburn and Clitheroe, along with a Bolton-based depot, stayed in Ribble ownership beyond deregulation day. Operations in Cumbria passed to Cumberland Motor services, while the Merseyside operations were passed to a new version of North Western.

The above reductions to the Ribble operation happened before 1986. By March 1988, Ribble was purchased by a management buy-out. This was followed by the 1989 Stagecoach purchase of the remaining Ribble area. By 2001 the depots based in Bolton, Blackburn, Clitheroe and Hyndburn were sold to Blazefield; the rest of the operation is still part of the Stagecoach North West/South Lancashire operational unit.

Blazefield introduced the blue and cream livery along with the Lancashire United (LU) name. The depot in Clitheroe was soon closed and this was followed by the closure of the Bolton depot. That part of LU was sold to Blue Bus of Howich, which later became part of Arriva.

In 2006 the LU unit passed to the French-owned Transdev, who purchased the Blackburn Transport fleet in 2007. Bringing the Spot-On livery and brand, by 2012 the Spot-On brand was replaced by the blue and yellow livery, the boulevard bus station was closed, and a new facility was opened during 2016. Today the Blackburn Bus Company continue with a two-tone blue livery. Based at the old Corporation Intack depot, with a low-floor fleet and new brands and new buses.

Bolton depot was a part of the Blazefield group for a short time as the services were passed to Blue Bus of Howich. 178 was new to Stagecoach in 1996. It is a Dennis Lance with Berkhof bodywork and is seen in the old Bolton bus station. Numbers 176–180 were all withdrawn by May 2002 and later sold on.

193 was part of a batch of Alexander-bodied Dennis Lance saloons, new in 1992 to East London. Numbers 181–196 were converted to single door before entering service with Stagecoach Ribble in 1997. Here, as Lancashire United 193, the bus is seen in Bolton working to Edgworth. As mentioned before, the Bolton depot was later sold to Blue Bus of Howich.

2095, a former Burnley & Pendle Alexander-bodied Bristol VRT, is seen pausing at the Blackburn bus station while it was moved to Manor Sutton Street depot in the town. With the influx of newer vehicles, this bus and other older models were withdrawn from service.

Eight former Manchester Alexander ALX200-bodied Volvo B6Bs were transferred to Burnley and Blackburn before the sale of the East Lancashire operations to Blazefield. Here 210 is seen working the Hyndburn Circular 6 and 7 service as the bus departs the bus station. 210 also sports the improved blue and cream livery quickly introduced to the fleet during 2001.

Thirty new Volvo B10BLEs with Wrightbus Renown bodywork were ordered for the Blackburn depot. Here 1076 is seen awaiting a driver and passengers on this former Ribble route, the Clitheroe to Bolton service. This route was later split into two, serving Clitheroe to Blackburn as the 22 and then Blackburn to Bolton, via Darwen, as the number 1.

1087 is seen working the Hyndburn services early in its career, as the bus was stationed at Blackburn. During 2007 the bus moved across to Burnley as part of the Mainline fleet. Two years later, in 2009, the bus moved to Harrogate to work the 770/771 Wetherby services, staying until 2018. It then moved to York and Burnley, where 1087 was repainted into the new two-tone orange Burnley livery in 2019.

The former Ribble service 152, which still runs today as the Hotline, has always been treated as a frontline service. Here 1101 is seen in Burnley, with Transdev fleetnames, working the 152 service with roof coving branding. The bus moved across to Burnley a few times until finally returning home to Blackburn in 2011, where 1101 is still working in the fleet.

1852 was new to Tyers Tours in 2005 and found its way across to Blackburn Manor Sutton Street during 2008. Here the bus is seen departing the old Blackburn Boulevard bus station, which today is pedestrianised. The Lancashire Way was the name for the express service to Manchester. 1852 was named as *Pride of Manchester*. Later, during 2012, the bus was repainted into the revised Spot-On livery but has since been withdrawn and sold.

In 1999 Blackburn Transport purchased a batch of five low-floor Volvo B10BLEs with Wrightbus Renown bodywork. These buses were painted into a pleasing green and cream livery with yellow swoops and easy access branding. By 2008 Blackburn was acquired by Transdev, who branded the whole operation as Spot-On. Here 206 is seen in the town working its way to Accrington on the number 1 service.

During 1999 a batch of ten Dennis Darts with Plaxton Pointer bodies arrived. These were later joined by six more in 2002. Blackburn Transport was acquired by Transdev in 2007, and soon found the fleet being turned into the Spot-On brand. Here 655 is seen passing the bus station, working the Sunnybower service, in the white and grey base scheme with the addition of turquoise to the front end.

To replace time-expired vehicles, Transdev placed into service a batch of Volvo B7RLEs with Wrightbus Eclipse bodies. Here 1825 is seen in the purple additional colour for the Spot-On theme working the Hyndburn 7 service. The bus moved to Keighley during early 2017. It was painted into a green livery for the Keighley Cougars rugby team. It was later renamed *Danny Jones* as a tribute to this popular player.

1840, which was new as a Volvo demonstrator, was acquired by Blackburn in 2007. Here the bus is seen arriving into Skipton, in April 2010, working the long 280 service from Preston, via Clitheroe and Barnoldswick. Later two vehicles, numbers 1841/42, were painted into the blue and yellow Blackburn livery and branded. In 2016 Preston bus won the contract to work the route and did so in two sections: the 280 Preston–Clitheroe and 180 Clitheroe–Skipton. However, from mid-June 2019, Preston decided to withdraw from operating the service. Stagecoach now operate this service with some reductions and revisions to the route.

2713 is seen departing Blackburn while working the X41, the Lancashire Way service. The livery is a copy of the 2003 36 livery, with the addition of the red rose of Lancashire. This bus was transferred across to Keighley during 2012 and has remained with Keighley ever since, gaining the blue and green 2010 livery before entering service.

During September 2010, eight integral Optare Tempo X1200s arrived for use on the 225 Clitheroe to Bolton service. Here 1306 is seen departing the bus station in Clitheroe, making its way back to Bolton, on 5 July 2011. In September 2012 the 225 was split into two sections: the 22 for the Blackburn–Clitheroe section and the 1 for the Blackburn–Bolton section. 1301–8 had all been withdrawn and returned off lease by October 2017.

Former Keighley Volvo B10B/Wrightbus Renown 573 is seen in what has to be one of the shortest used liveries: the improved Spot-On style. Here the bus is leaving on the 6 service to Accrington, part of the former Hyndburn Circular services route. Since this photo, 573 has been rebranded for the 2017 Valleyline 22 service.

1098 is seen in Preston working the 152 service back to Burnley, via Blackburn, in the new yellow and blue livery. 1098 also has additional branding for the service along its roof coving panels. The 152 was to undergo a few changes in 2016 with a new livery, brand and improved vehicles along the service.

402 has enjoyed a varied and busy life, starting with Yorkshire Coastliner in the summer of 2004 in the indigo livery. By 2010 the bus was repainted into the brighter two-tone blue livery and moved across to Harrogate in December 2010. After the 36 City Connect programme was finished, 402 found its way to Blackburn, as seen here with the bus in Manchester working the X41, the Lancashire Way. By April 2017, 402 was again returning to Yorkshire, as part of the Keighley Bus Company fleet.

As part of the new fresh image for the Blackburn Bus Company, eighteen new Optare Versa saloons were purchased for the very popular 6 and 7 Accrington Circular service. Here 221 travels along Thwaites Road, heading towards Accrington on the 7, in September 2016. Since then, including the Blackburn batch, over seventy-six Optare Versas have entered service with new and improved passenger comforts, such as free Wi-Fi, USB power, wireless charging, tables, glazed roofs and new seating with better legroom.

The Blackburn 22 service also gained an image refresh as the improved Valley line, which saw revitalised buses enter service in the spring of 2017. Here the former Keighley bus 566 arrives into Clitheroe in May 2017, looking very smart in the new dark blue and yellow livery.

The Red Express arrived during 2016, taking over the Lancashire Way X41 service with a brand refresh. Here is a former 36 Twindeck vehicle, number 3602, one of seven vehicles appointed to the route. Here 3602 is seen between Blackburn and Accrington while working an afternoon duty on the service in September 2016. The Red Express was revised during 2018 and now terminates in Accrington instead of Blackburn.

Former WitchWay 2760 is seen in Blackburn working the 152 Hotline, returning to Burnley, in early 2018. The Hotline was officially launched in September 2017 in both Blackburn and Preston. 2756–62 are in the dedicated Hotline two-tone purple livery along with route branding; Pride of the North liveried 2754–55 work as cover for the service.

1865, a former Burnley Mainline fleet vehicle, was repainted into the Blackburn Bus Company livery and given new seats, USB power sockets and free Wi-Fi. 1863 and 1864 were also repainted and given the same interior fixtures and fittings, while 1866 and 1867 were painted into the new Pride of the North livery. Here 1865 is seen working the number one service between Blackburn and Bolton via Darwen. These revitalised buses joined the 2012 batch of Volvo/Wrightbus saloons, 1872–78, on the service. At the time of writing, an order of thirteen ADL E20Ds, with enhanced Transdev features and environmentally friendly engines, will be arriving in 2020.

Yorkshire Coastliner

January 1990 saw an old name being used for the east coast service, as AJS brought the Yorkshire Coastliner name back. This time, like the 1984 West Yorkshire Road Car express services for the east coast, the services are based in Malton. Initially using former West Yorkshire vehicles, Leyland Leopards and Olympians, new buses arrived in 1992, with six Northern Counties-bodied Olympians mixing with other vehicles. 1994 brought in the first Alexander Royale-bodied Volvo Olympians, with four newer examples following in 1995.

The operational area was the same as in 1984, with services starting in Leeds, then York, via Tadcaster. Then they headed into Malton where passengers could change for services to Whitby, Filey and Bridlington and Scarborough. 1996 saw the first five low-floor Volvo B10BLE saloons arrive, followed by one more B10BLE and four more Volvo Olympians in 1997. The last seven longer Volvo Olympians arrived in 2000, these being the final Royales built. 2002 brought in four B10Bs and three Plaxton B7TLs. From 2004 the standard double-deckers would be the Wright Gemini B7TLs, with a batch of six B7RLEs arriving in 2005. New Volvo deckers arrived in 2006, 2008, 2011 and 2014.

However, in early December 2016, the first of ten brand new Volvo B5TLs were showcased at York Minster. The rest arrived into service soon after, with three more arriving during 2018. Today the routes service Scarborough and Whitby but continue to serve Bridlington during the summer months.

New in 1980 to WYRCC as their 2582 is this Plaxton-bodied Leyland Leopard, which joined the new Yorkshire Coastliner operation in April 1990. After being withdrawn in 1994, 466 was passed briefly to Harrogate but was soon sold. Like all of the buses initially used at Malton, all were from the York City & District fleet.

Leeds Central bus station lay-over area sees 481 (1859), one of the original ten WYRCC NBC Yorkshire Coastliner buses. 1850–59 were coach-seated Olympians painted into a two-tone blue Venetian blind stylised livery. The bus would gain route branding during 1992.

1992 saw the delivery of six Northern Counties-bodied Leyland Olympians; these would be the last new Leylands purchased by Coastliner as Volvo acquired Leyland in 1993. Here 402, the first of the batch, is seen in York working its way towards Stonebow bound for Scarborough.

1990 saw the arrival of five new Leyland Tiger coaches with Plaxton bodywork to improve the saloon coaching fleet. 432 is seen paused in Leeds while on 843 duty. It would later join the Keighley fleet after its withdrawal from Coastliner in 1996.

Taking in some later evening autumnal sunshine is 409, one of two new Volvo Olympians with striking Alexander Royale bodies. 408/9 arrived in 1994 and were soon at home on the Coastliner routes. Both were withdrawn in June 2000 and were moved across to Harrogate. Later, both buses were acquired by Geldard's of Leeds.

Yorkshire Coastliner regularly replaced and updated the fleet, keeping the operation one of the youngest fleets in the UK for many a year. Here is 453, one of five new Volvo B10Bs which were placed into service during early 1996. Here 453 is seen on Rougier Street, York, heading for Leeds, having done a Whitby run. 451–55 were later moved on to Lancashire United in 2002.

Yorkshire Coastliner replaced three 1992 Leyland Olympians with four more Volvo Olympians with Alexander Royale bodies, new in 1995. Here, 423, the second of the batch, is seen in Leeds working the 843 to Scarborough. 422–5 were later transferred to Keighley in 2000, for use on the main 760 service.

Yorkshire Coastliner continues with the stylish Alexander Royale-bodied Volvo Olympians. Four more joined in 1997 as 426–9. 426, pictured in Station Road opposite the railway station during a sunny afternoon, is bound for Leeds. In 2003, 426–429 were transferred across to Lancashire United, later joined by 427 after its visit to London-based Sovereign.

Yorkshire Coastliner purchased 441 in 2001, the only new bus to arrive in that year. A sunny Malton Railway Street is the location for this shot of 441, working the long 840 service to Whitby. 441 soon found its way to Lancashire United in 2005, during which time it was renumbered to 1041. It moved to Harrogate (2006), then Keighley (2007) and back to Harrogate in 2010. The bus was reseated to B57F for the schools fleet as Keighley beckoned in 2013. 1041 returned to Harrogate in 2017.

Yorkshire Coastliner took the final UK-built Alexander Royale-bodied Olympians in 2000 with seven examples, 431–7. 434 is seen parked outside the Peasholm Park stop. This area has changed across the years with redevelopment. This batch was withdrawn in 2006 and ended working with First Bus. These were the last Volvo Olympians to be built, after which the B7TL low-floor chassis became the standard.

In 2002 the first low-floor double-deckers arrived at Malton in the shape of the Volvo B7TL with Plaxton President bodywork. 438, the first of the trio of vehicles, is seen on the Railway Road entrance to the depot at Malton, looking smart after delivery. Upon withdrawal from Coastliner, in 2008, 438–440 were transferred to Lancashire United. 438 was moved to Keighley in 2012 and 439 and 440 joined Keighley in 2017.

Yorkshire Coastliner took five low-floor Volvo B10BLEs into stock in 2002, initially 442–5, joined, in May, by 446 with a Preston plate. Here 443 is seen having just entered service, working the 842 to Thornton Le Dale with full branding for the east coast routes. 443 returned to York as 1013 and was used on the Unibus route until withdrawal in 2017.

As the thirty-six Twindecks settled in Harrogate, Yorkshire Coastliner acquired their first Volvo B7TL/Gemini double-deckers. In the spring of 2004, 401–4 arrived in a new indigo and blue livery for the east coast routes. 401 is seen in York in August 2004 collecting several passengers. After a yearlong move to Harrogate, in 2010, the bus moved to Blackburn in 2012. In 2019 the bus was used to celebrate the Ribble 100.

Early 2006 saw six more Volvo B7TL/WrightBuses enter service in the new indigo livery, numbered 405–410. Here 407 is seen departing Tadcaster working the 840 to Thornton Le Dale on a sunny 11 May 2009. Upon withdrawal, 407 saw further service across the Pennines at Lancashire United. It joined 405–6 and 408 as part of the Lancashire Way brand.

Ten improved Volvo B9TLs with Wrightbus Gemini bodywork arrived in early 2008, with 'Forest and Fens' Nottingham registration plates. 411–420 were considered by many of the Coastliner drivers to be the best vehicles on the east coast routes. Here 414 is seen passing the former West Yorkshire Vicar Lane bus station, heading for the Leeds bus station on 11 May 2009.

April 2011 saw four more smartly turned out Volvo B9TL/Wrightbus Gemini 2-bodied vehicles arrive. Here the first of the batch is seen on the A64 York Road, Leeds, starting the long journey towards Bridlington on the 845. 421 was withdrawn in early 2017 but was soon repainted into the Pride of the North livery. It debuted on 10 April 2017, on the X43 Manchester to Skipton service.

Following the four brand-new Volvo B9TL/Wrightbus Gemini 2s, 2013 brought another five new double-deckers into Coastliner stock. 425–429 were painted, just like 421–424, in the much brighter two-tone blue 2010 livery. 429 is depicted here heading along the A64 York Road, working an early evening return to Leeds. The last of these B9TLs will be replaced no doubt by another batch of Volvo B5/Wrightbus Gemini 3s.

December 2016 saw 3631 and 3632 arrive into York and park outside York Minster for the first public display of the ten new high-specification Volvo B5TLs with Wright Gemini 3 bodies. Unlike the 36, the upper saloon seats have a cloth cover with e-leather sections. Two tables were also placed in the upper saloon, with 13-amp plug sockets and USB power across the vehicle. The lower saloon also had the same rear layout as the 36, with a table and USB power instead of seats facing the rear seating. Here 3630 is seen leaving the long climb out of Goathland, heading towards Whitby, on 24 March 2017.

York 2008–18 York & Country 2018

Transdev made a return into York during 2008, having successfully acquired the Veolia bus operations. The former Fulford depot was taken as well, keeping vehicles secure. York also took over the stage carriage work of York Pullman during 2012, including the very popular 44 Unibus service.

The York operation initially ran buses in the Veolia red and grey livery, but soon a two-tone blue livery was created in 2009 along with a brand-new service, the 844. This was based on the Coastliner scheme. A lighter version was on the remaining stage carriage work vehicles.

York had expanded its routes serving Fulford, Monks Cross and two routes into Skelton. But even with these services in operation, the tender renewal across the years has seen a much-reduced fleet at the York depot.

Apart from the Unibus service, which the contract was later won by First York, the biggest success saw the new CityZap express service introduced in 2016. Since then the route has brought beyond 250,000 customers on board. The former United routes of the 56/57 and 142/143, which have seen many changes since 2010, were merged in 2016 to become the Little Explorers.

A new two-tone blue livery was introduced along with a new brand for the York depot in 2018, York & Country, as the news of the collapse of Stephensons of Easingwold in January 2018 was revealed. The brand has also seen younger Optare Versa buses being transferred from Harrogate and repainted into the two-tone blue livery.

New to Alton Towers transport in 2005, then to Veolia in 2007, and then to Top Line in 2008, was 1262, an integral Optare Solo M920, seen here working a York local service 14 on 11 May 2009. York continued with the Veolia red and grey livery until the middle of 2009, when the new blue livery was introduced.

As a direct response to the First West Yorkshire X64 service, York registered the 844. The route served the same route as the First service but extended to Heworth. Six former Blackburn Spot-On Optare Versas were transferred and repainted into a single-deck version of the Coastliner livery. Here 272 is seen picking up passengers on the first day of operation on 11 May 2009.

The 2005 batch of Yorkshire Coastliner Volvo B7RLEs was split in March 2008; numbers 450–2 went to Harrogate and 453–55 to Keighley. Here 450 is seen on Rouiger Street, York, having transferred across to York during 2009. Again, the bus is depicted in the single-deck livery that was introduced for the 844. Currently 450 is based at Keighley and was revitalised in 2015 with Transdev features and Eclipse 2 front end. It was also painted into the Keighley duo green livery.

1054, a former Burnley Mainline vehicle new in 2001, is seen here in central York working the 14 service. 1054 ventured to Harrogate in 2009 then moved to York in 2010. The bus then became part of the Unibus 44 operation from York Pullman in 2012, staying until withdrawn in July 2017. It was the last bus in the Unibus livery.

New to Dublin bus then moving to Veolia Transport in 2007, by 2008 this bus became 2002 in the York fleet. During the summer of 2011, York operated a direct service via Malton to Flamingo Land: the 840. 2002 is seen in York, working the first full through service to the activity resort. The bus was moved across to Burnley during 2013.

Former Harrogate 605 was transferred to York during 2011 and quickly repainted into the two-tone blue livery. Here 605 exits Piccadilly, in York, bound for Skelton in late November 2011. Reliance of Stockton on the Forest gained the 19B and 19L during late 2013. The bus had a short stay in York and was sold during 2012.

New to Blackburn in 2007, 1835 was moved across to York during 2012 and is seen here working the 19L from Skelton. However, by 2014 the batch of Blackburn 2007 Volvo B7RLEs, 1816/22/24/26/29/32–3/35 and 36 were sold to Rossendale in 2014 as 141–9. The bus returned to Transdev in 2018 as 1733 and is now part of the revitalised Irwell Line service.

276 was the only former Blackburn Spot-On Optare Versa to be painted into the two-tone blue livery. Here 276 is seen on Station Rise in York working the former York Pullman service 26 to Tesco. During late 2013 the 26 was lost to Arriva after the tender was offered. In 2019, York will again operate the route as the tender was gained for the 24, 25 and 26 from Arriva.

York Pullman had formed a large base for the 44 Unibus service, which was proving popular with the university students. However, the service was placed out to tender in 2012 so two former London double-deckers were converted to single door. Here 2718, new to London Central as PVL269, is seen working the service in York. After the loss of the Unibus service to First York, 2718 was moved across to Keighley in 2016.

Yorkshire Coastliner's penultimate batch of saloons arrived in 2002 and were the last Volvo B10BLEs made for the UK. Here 1013, formerly 443, is seen on Station Rise, in York, working the 44 Unibus service. 1013 arrived at Blackburn in May 2005, moving to York in 2012 in time for the Unibus switchover, where it was painted into the new livery.

New to Dunn Line, then a part of Veolia group, was this short Optare Solo M880 that transferred across to York. Here the bus is seen in York as 1264, working the 24 service. As previously mentioned, the 24–6 services were later acquired by Arriva in 2013 as the services were placed for tender. The Optare Solos were so replaced by Volvo B7RLEs saloons during 2012/13, as the services were all placed to tender, with York gaining the 36, briefly, and the 44 Unibus services.

New to York Pullman in September 2010, 1107, along with sister vehicle 1106, passed to Transdev York in 2012. Here the bus is seen exiting Rouiger Street into Station Rise during a bright sunny day, in the full Unibus livery. Since the university route contract was won by First in 2016, 1107 has been repainted into the York blue livery. In 2019 the bus moved to Burnley.

Two former Nottingham City Transport Scania Omnicity CN94UBs (529–30) were placed on loan as 1109–10 from April 2015. Here 1110 is seen on Station Rise having exited Rouiger Street whilst working the 142 York to Ripon via Boroughbridge service. The route was once operated by United until October 1996, when Harrogate acquired and operated it until 2010. The routes returned in 2015. By 2016 the 56/57/142 and 143 were combined as Little Explorers.

This Volvo B10BLE/Wrightbus was new to Yorkshire Coastliner as 445 in 2002, moving to Lancashire United during 2005. By 2009 the bus had returned to York to be painted in the Veolia red and grey livery. However, after some time during 2011, and now numbered 1015, the bus was repainted into the 2010 brighter Coastliner livery. It is seen here on Clifford Street, on 23 February 2016, working the special Tadfaster service as the bridge in Tadcaster was damaged during the 2015 Boxing Day floods. Thankfully the bridge was repaired and reopened in early 2017 – a relief to the people of the town. Yorkshire Coastliner named 3635 *The Spirt of Tadcaster* in honor of the town.

1059 is seen in Micklegate, York, working the final few days of the 44 Unibus service in early 2016, before Transdev withdrew from competing with First York's 66 service. Having grown the service, Transdev placed the 44 as a twenty-four-hour service, operating from late 2014. During early 2019, 1059 made her one-way trip to the scrap man.

CityZap arrived in March 2016, having been in the pipeline for a few months, using five former 36 City Connect 'Twindeck' vehicles from Harrogate. The York to Leeds service was highly successful, bringing in over 250,000 customers during its first year of operation, plus a 97 per cent customer satisfaction rating. However, during early 2019 two demonstrator vehicles were evaluated on the route – one Wrightbus Streetdeck and an ADL E40D MMC. In November 2019, two tri-axle coaches – one Mercedes Benz and an Irizar integral – were both tried for a week each on the route, with the results to be made known in 2020.

As mentioned on page 81 the new Little Explorers were launched during 2016, using three former Keighley Trans-bus Darts. These were made from combining the 56/57 Boroughbridge, and the 142/143 Ripon to York via Boroughbridge services. Here 714, the last of the trio, is seen in Littlethorpe, a village just outside of Ripon, working the 23 back to York. 706/707 and 714 were later transferred across to Rosso Bus in 2018, as the York fleet was again evolving into York & Country.

In 2017 York had taken over the 42 service, a route operated by Arriva, using a mixture of vehicles. In 2018 two dealer stock ADL E20Ds arrived (726 and 727) and were placed into service. Here, 726 exits Stillingfleet on its way to Selby. During early 2019 the 42 was placed for tender and Arriva regained the service.

Former Harrogate 211, new in 2012 as 281, is seen here working the 194 Hovingham to Malton service. This route was acquired following the unexpected collapse of North Yorkshire-based Stephensons of Easingwold. Currently as York & Country, the 181 Castle Howard (now the Castle Line in 2019) and the 194 Hovingham routes are served.

New changes happened in York on Saturday 31 August, when newly tendered services were operated after being awarded to Transdev. This saw the Fulford depot operating the 24 Acomb, 25 Derwenthopre, and the 26 Fulford and south bank services again after losing them in 2013 to Arriva Yorkshire. York also gained the evening working on the 14 Haxby to York along with the Saturday workings of the 19 York to Skelton route. Here 753 is seen arriving into Crossfield Crescent during the first Monday of operation on the new routes. With thanks to the driver for being able to get this shot.

Rossendale/Rosso Bus 2013

Both Rawtenstall and Haslingden corporations commenced operations from 1907 using motor buses. During 1968, both undertakings agreed to a merging of operations, forming the Rossendale Joint Transport committee. With the 1972 local government reorganisation the boundaries changed, with Bacup and Whitworth joining the new Rossendale Borough in 1974.

The 1985 Transport Act again saw some change to Rossendale, as the council links became an arm's length structure. This led to the 2009 demonstrations, as the rumors of a sale of the company were heard. By July 2009, after proceedings found the council could retain the bus company, much to the relief of local passengers, services continued.

The late summer of 2013 saw a major brand refresh, with a new, brighter livery, and new name Rosso Bus. This was a much-needed change, which led to an interesting period in December 2017, as French-owned bus operator Transdev had entered into negotiations with the council for the company.

2018 turned out to be a very busy year for Rosso Bus with internal and external improvements, with a deal secured with the promise of a £3 million investment of sixteen new buses for the 464. Revitalised vehicles were brought in for the new Tottington Line, Red4, Lakeline, Irwell Line and Trax across the year. Buses were transferred across the network to Burnley and Blackburn depots, as the Haslingden depot was not part of the sale. The whole network has grown since the purchase, with a much-improved performance for Rosso Bus.

New to Lothian, this Leyland Lynx was a secondhand purchase by Rossendale in 2000 as number 180. Here the bus is paused at the former Bolton bus station, about to head for Rawtenstall on the 273.

New to Mayne of Manchester is this rather unique Marshall Dartline C37 body on the very popular Dennis Dart chassis, pictured in 1999. Here the bus is seen in Blackburn working the 236 service; the bus arrived into stock in 1998. 129 arrived with three more vehicles from Maynes, all in the same style as 129.

The Easyride branding and livery were the Rossendale low-floor format. Here 152, a Wrightbus-bodied Volvo B7RLE, is seen parked up awaiting another turn on the 464 Rochdale to Accrington service. This bus did pass to Transdev when the company was acquired in late 2017.

During 2013 Rossendale was given a major brand refresh, with a new shorter name and a brighter livery. Here is 2732, a former Metroline Volvo B7TL/Plaxton that arrived into the Rosso bus fleet in 2013. The bus is seen working the 466 service to Todmorden from Bacup. Since this picture was taken, the bus has moved to the Keighley schools fleet. The 466 was renumbered as the 8 in 2019.

Here another Wrightbus-bodied Volvo B7RLE is seen working in Bury town centre on the 484. This route was one of many Rosso bus routes which have been revitalised with improved buses, standard features from Transdev along with bold liveries, catchy advertisements, slogans and new timetables.

During 2018 the Streetlites based at Keighley were transferred across to Rosso for a programme of revitalised services. Here, 610 is seen at the Tottington line route terminus in the new-look livery and branding for the 469. 610 is joined by 618 and 619, both from Wrightbus dealer stock; these are integral Streetlites.

The Lakeline is the new brand for the 456 and 458 services, which have seen plenty of improvements in the revitalised Streetlites and passenger growth. 612–615, all four new to Rosso in 2016, are used for the Lakeline service. Here, 614 is seen in the town of Littleborough, departing on the 458 towards Rochdale via Illingworth lake.

With the closure of the CityZap Manchester service, 1868–71 were repainted and given a new role for the Rosso bus operation. Here 1871 is seen in Bury, operating back to Ramsbottom as the Red4. The Red4 replaces the former 484 service. Again, the new look has brought vehicles with a host of Transdev features such as improved legroom, free Wi-Fi, USB power and the new image on the buses and timetables.

The promise of a brand-new investment of eighteen new buses for the trunk 464 service arrived in October 2018. The bold purple livery and bright branding saw the new Optare Versa saloons arrive in style. The new buses were showcased in various parts of the 464 routes, which saw interested passengers looking at the new buses. Here 283 is seen passing through Stacksteads during the first morning of operation, looking very smart in the 464 livery.

The next service to gain the revitalised image was the 481 and 483 Irwell Line services between Bury and Rawtenstall. They received hourly extensions to Blackburn (481) and to Burnley (483), with numbers 1726–33 branded for the new-look image. Here 1728 is seen climbing towards Waterfoot, working the 13:17 run from Burnley to Bury, during the first Monday of full operation of the Irwell Line service on 28 January 2019.

A former Burnley-based Wrightbus Streetlite is seen in Bury, while working the 467 Bury to Rochdale service. Trax is the new name for the Rochdale/Bury link (467/468 services). 601–9 and 611 are used on the Trax services, as illustrated by 601 working the 467 towards Rochdale. 616–7 are painted into a two-tone yellow spare livery for the Rochdale services.

The promise of revitalised buses for the Rosso bus fleet continues, as vehicles are slowly given overhauls with new interior fixtures and fittings and a new fresh livery. 1715 is paused in busy peak time traffic, outside of Bury, during late October 2019. The bus is one of three new to Minsterley Motors, Stiperstones, in March 2012. They moved to Rossendale in 2015.

Rosso Bus replaced several older former London Volvo/Plaxton deckers, which were transferred across to Keighley for school contracts routes. These are ADL E40Ds, former London vehicles, new to Metroline in 2007; they arrived and had a quick tidy round and were numbered 2811–18. Here the last of the batch, 2818, is seen in Bury.

Demonstration Duties

In September 2018 a new vehicle was loaned to Harrogate for what turned out to be just over a year's loan. Volvo had replaced the B7RLE chassis with a new Euro IV model, the B8RLE, with plenty of options for bodywork. Here, 1900 is seen working the 21, the 14:55 to Roecliffe, in September 2019. The bus has a new-look body by MCV, the EvoRa, which arrived in a white livery. The decals were added a week or so later.

The Optare Metrocity saloon has been on an extended loan to Transdev. This particular example has been with Transdev since September 2018, and was formerly with Rosso, Blackburn and then Burnley. The bus was seen as number 300 in April 2019 while working the Pike Hill service. This bus also has the new Alison xFE type gearbox, which is used with a Euro IV Mercedes Benz engine.

Shaping the future for passengers in Blackburn travelling to Bolton was this smart looking ADL E20D MMC demonstration bus used in September 2019. Here number 301 is seen working the route while on hire. For delivery in early 2020 are thirteen high-specification versions of the ADL, each with the usual Transdev passenger comforts: new seats, USB power, wireless charging, next stop announcements and Wi-Fi.

The Aireline 60, which follows the River Aire on its journey into Leeds, was seeing increased passengers on the early peak time duties. A solution was sought and this new Wrightbus Streetdeck was tried for a couple of weeks in December 2018. Here as 302 on the books, the bus is seen in Rodley, Leeds, working an afternoon rota on the service.

This striking long wheelbase version of the ADL E40D MMC was used by York in early 2019. It was loaned for a few days for evaluation of the CityZap service and had the 6.7-litre Cummins engine coupled to a ZX 6-speed eco-life gearbox. The bus gained good reviews from passengers and drivers. 302 is seen in York having arrived from Leeds. Later in November 2019, two tri-axle coaches were evaluated for the service, pending a final decision on an order for 2020 delivery.

The 36 service in Harrogate saw investment in 2015 with an order for fourteen long wheelbase Volvo B5TLs with the new Wrightbus Gemini 3 bodywork. Seen here working the route in January 2015 is this former demonstrator, which had a six-month spell in Dublin. It was acquired by East Yorkshire in 2016. Here the bus is seen on the main A61 Ripon Road near the village of Ripley, a popular tourist destination.

To finish the book, the Keighley Bus Company registered the summer Dales Bus service 821, which visits the historic town of Pateley Bridge and then goes on to Scar House Reservoir. The area is popular with walkers and tourists, as is the town of Pateley Bridge, where the 821 visits again. It also operates two daily trips to Otley.